How to Handle Cowards, Thieves, Liars and Manipulators Without Breaking The Law

By K.C. Smith

Table of Contents

Introduction

In the classic Disney Snow White, the main character didn't make her journey through life alone. She had a host of people to accompany her, including an evil, vindictive, jealous witch and seven diligent miners all with their own distinct characters. If you've watched the movie you probably remember some of them, Sneezy, Dopey, Sleepy and Grumpy. Interesting names right? Says a lot about the kind of people she had to deal with.

In this journey we call life, like Snow White we have an entire host of characters that we have to travel with. You might not have to deal with a witch, but there is a high chance that you will meet people who are vindictive and jealous. While the majority of the people we come across in our daily lives or the people we have to live and work with are going to be happy and decent, there are going to be some people who have all the characteristics of the witch and then some!

Burdensome, rude, disrespectful, demanding – these are just a few adjectives to describe some of the distasteful characters we have to deal with daily. I have no doubt that you have picked up this book because you are dealing with someone or some people in your life who are just as the title describes, manipulative, thieves, liars and cowards! Maybe it's a miserable boss, a co-worker or a friend, family member or loved one. Regardless of who the person is, you feel as if you are at your wits end and you want to know how to deal with them more effectively.

I am a firm believer in karma, whatever you put out comes right back to you. When you are dealing with people of this caliber what you really want to do is give them a piece of your mind! But what is that going to achieve? ABSOLUTELY NOTHING! You will end up reducing yourself to their level and feeling worse than before you started your revenge mission and bring bad luck your way.

Sometimes we are unable to put our finger on exactly what the problem is, there is just something about that person that makes them difficult to get along with. Whether the people we meet or the people we try to avoid work for us or against us is purely down to how we handle them. There are plenty of excellent reference books that explain the psychology behind people's behavior. While we will look at some of these issues briefly, that is not the focus of this book. Our focus is on how to deal with such people in a way that is not going to get you into any trouble. In this book we are going to look at how to handle cowards, thieves, liars and manipulators without breaking the law.

Chapter 1: What is Manipulation?

There is nothing wrong with wanting to get your needs met, but people who are manipulative use indirect, deceptive and abusive methods to get people to do things for them. Manipulation can appear innocent or even flattering or friendly. You will feel as if the person has your best interests at heart but everything they do or say has an ulterior motive behind it.

If you were raised in a manipulative household, you will find it difficult to discern when you are being manipulated because what is taking place doesn't feel uncomfortable; it is behavior that is normal to you. You may feel a sense of anger or discomfort, but manipulators use reasonable and pleasant language. They play on your sympathy or your guilt so that you ignore your instincts and end up agreeing to their demands. People who are co-dependent are particularly vulnerable to being manipulated because they don't know how to be assertive and may even use manipulation tactics to get what they want.

Some of a manipulators favorite tactics include: guilt, lying, complaining, denying, comparing, rationalizing, making excuses, feigning innocence or ignorance, bribery, blame, mind games, undermining, getting their foot in the door, reversals, evasiveness, emotional blackmail, gifts, flattery, and favors. Manipulators will often use guilt tactics by saying things such as, "After everything I've done for you," or behaving in a chronically helpless or needy way. They may compare you in a negative way to someone else by saying, "You are just like your father," who is an abusive alcoholic. They will bring other people that don't exist into the argument and use them as allies by saying things like "You are selfish, everyone says that about you."

Some manipulators will make a promise, an agreement or have a conversation with you about something important and then deny that any of it took place. They will start an argument about it and blame you for something that has nothing to do with you to get you to feel sorry for them and to wield power over you. This is the approach they will use to break an agreement, or a promise or to deny that they had a certain conversation with you. Parents who manipulate their children do so with bribery, "If you finish your dinner you can have desert, "No playing with your video games until you get your homework done." Depending on the type of bribe that you agree to, it can undermine your self-respect.

Manipulators will often use the tone of your voice and make assumptions about your beliefs or intentions and then react to their imaginary assumptions as if they were true. They then use this to justify their behavior at the same time as denying what was actually said in the conversation. They will act as if you agreed or decided upon something and ignore any objections or input that you may have. When you object to their demands, they make you out to be the bad guy and they are the innocent victims. They have now turned the focus onto them and their complaints which is what they wanted in the first place. They will often pretend as if they are concerned or worried about you and this is often used to undermine your confidence in certain decisions you have made.

Emotional blackmail is an abusive manipulation tactic and it may include the use of intimidation, rage threats, guilt or shame. They will make you doubt yourself and feel insecure through shame, they often disguise this as a complaint by saying things such as, "I am shocked that someone of your caliber can stoop to such levels!" A typical tactic is to scare you with threats, accusations, anger or warnings such as, "You are too old to meet anyone now, you will be alone for the rest of your life if you leave, or "You will never find anyone better than me," or they will play the victim role and say things like, "I can't live without you."

People who use blackmail will often attempt to scare you with anger so that you sacrifice your needs and wants. If they are unsuccessful, they reduce their intensity to calm you down and get you to agree with what they want you to do. They might bring up something from your past that you feel ashamed or guilty about to threaten you. They will say things like, "I will tell your sister about abc, if you don't do xyz."

People who are passive aggressive are also very manipulative. They don't know how to be assertive and so they will say what they think the other person wants to hear to be loved or to prevent conflict, but they will still go ahead and do what they want. A passive aggressive person does not answer questions that they feel will lead to confrontation, they will be evasive or change the subject or use denial or blame to avoid being seen as the person in the wrong. They find it difficult to say no, so they will say yes but then complain about how hard it is to fulfill the request they have agreed to.

When a passive aggressive is confronted about something they have done, they find it hard to accept responsibility, so they play the blame game, make apologies they don't mean or make excuses to keep the peace. They use flattery, charm and offer their help, favors and gifts for acceptance and love. Guilt, criticism, and self pity are used to manipulate so they can get what they want. They will say things like, "Why are you so selfish? All you think about is yourself, you never help me with my problems and I have spent all this time helping you." Playing the role of the victim is a way of manipulating others through guilt.

Passive aggressive behavior is a way of expressing hostility, because you are not assertive enough to say no, you will get out of doing it by being late or conveniently forgetting that you had agreed to the task, this is often a way of expressing anger.

Addicts will lie and deny to manipulate and protect their addiction. Their partners or family members will also participate in the manipulation by hiding or diluting the addict's alcohol or drugs. To control the addict's behavior, they will tell half truths or lie to avoid confrontation or to control the addict's behavior.

Chapter 2: How to Disarm a Manipulative Person

You are reading this chapter because you read the chapter before and recognized that you are being manipulated and you now want to know how you can effectively handle this individual without killing them! Well keep reading and you will find out, here are some steps to disarm a manipulative personality for good.

Don't Show Any Emotion

A manipulative person is led by your emotions; they are very observant creatures and pay close attention to your every move. Your emotions are like fuel, it's what keeps them running and without it they have nothing to work with. Here is how to interact with a manipulative person and show no emotion:

- Keep your conversation to a minimum; only say what needs to be said. In other words be direct and to the point.

- Make sure you are never the main topic of conversation; the less they know about you the better.
- Avoid using "we" and "I" in the conversation; you don't want the manipulator to feel like you are a team.

Ask them a lot of Questions

It can be difficult not to talk about yourself in a conversation and the manipulator knows this which is why they tend to ask a lot of questions. This is where you flip the script on them. The first thing is to provide a limited amount of information, if you can get away with it, give them a one word answer followed by a question. Don't ask a closed question, ask them something that involves them speaking about how they feel. For example if they ask you how you are doing today, say "Great" and then say "You are looking a bit pale, is everything alright with you? Have you been feeling ill lately?" This will totally catch them off guard because a manipulative person doesn't expect to talk about how they feel. They want their victim to expose themselves and open up so that they become vulnerable. When you ask a manipulator a personal question, you will see very quickly how reluctant they are to share intimate information unless they can use it to their advantage.

Point Out their Weak Points

Narcissists and manipulators have several things in common, and one of them is that they don't take criticism well. They present themselves as charming and appealing and anyone who can see their flaws is not the kind of person they want to try and manipulate. Point out their flaws in a casual and non confrontational manner, you can even laugh at it to make what you are doing appear less threatening. For example, midway through conversation you can say something like "I'm sorry to cut in, but do you realize you have a slight lisp? It's actually really cute, can you say that again." Then start laughing.

Manipulators like to bully people, they are used to playing the "alpha" role, and when someone points out one of their flaws, it completely throws them off track. Doing this with a sense of humor and courage will change their perception of you, they will realize that you are not someone they can walk over and that you will bite back.

Add Small Talk to the Conversation

When you are having a conversation with a manipulator, never talk about how you feel, don't discuss anything substantial with them. You should limit your conversation to subjects such as sports, celebrity gossip, politics and the weather. Regardless of the topic, they will keep trying to get you to open up, if you are talking about the weather, they will say something like, "It's really cloudy today, it's depressing when the weather is like this don't you agree?" You can easily shut a question like this down with wit and say something like, "Clouds look like gigantic cotton balls!"

Manipulators don't like small talk; they don't have anything to gain from it. They don't do anything for the sake of it, everything a manipulator does has to have a purpose, there must be something in it for them.

Just Say No

Manipulators don't understand the word "no," it's not in their vocabulary. They see it as an obstacle that they need to get around. However, if you keep on saying no the manipulator will move on to their next victim because they don't have time to waste, they want what they want and they want it now.

Give Them the Leftovers

A manipulator wants to get something out of you and they typically won't leave you alone until they get it. So if you have to give them something, give them the lowest quality possible and disappoint them. They will soon move on and find someone else who can be of more value to them.

Trust Your own Judgement

When you are confident and assertive it is difficult for people to manipulate you. You shouldn't need to ask anyone if you are good enough, or if you should make a certain decision in your life. You should know deep within who you are and what you need to do to get you where you want to go in life. Stop expecting other people to define you and define yourself. You need to learn how to trust your own judgement. What separates the winners from the losers is having the ability to hold onto your own belief system without compromise. When you have a made up mind about who you are and what you are prepared to tolerate the manipulator will not be able to get a foothold in your life.

Be Inconsistent

This is not what it sounds like, let me explain myself! It is a misconception that consistency is tied to success. The idea of success is that you keep growing, that you keep reinventing yourself. In other words you are not predictable, today you are a New York Times bestselling author, you are working towards your next goal and tomorrow your book has been made into a film. Success is about progression, you never remain on the same level. This constant movement is not consistent because people never know what you are going to do next.

Manipulative people thrive on consistency so that you can get what they need completed. They want you to be at home every day at a certain time so that you can cook the dinner and clean the house before they get back from work. Manipulators keep their victims in a box through consistency, the fact that they know what you are going to do next is a way of controlling you.

Don't try and fit in, instead make a conscious effort to be a non conformist in every area of your life; don't stay the same for too long. By definition, personal growth requires that you are inconsistent and that you are constantly reinventing yourself.

Refuse to Compromise

Guilt is a powerful weapon that the manipulator will use to get you to do what they want. They will make you feel guilty for past mistakes and small failures, or they will make you feel guilty for being proud of your achievements or for having confidence in yourself. To dampen your mood, they will say things like, "You should never be too confident, you never know what can happen next in your life."

In combination with guilt, they will also use doubt against you. They will make every effort to instill a sense of self doubt within you so that you are not certain about the skills and the abilities that you possess. Their main goal is to cause you to feel uncertain about yourself so that they can gain a stronger influence over you. When they have this kind of hold over your life you are more likely to compromise your beliefs, goals and values.

The solution here is quite simple, don't allow them to make you feel guilty and don't allow them to make you lose your confidence in who you are and your abilities. You don't owe anything to anyone and you have the right to feel proud of what you have achieved. It is very self destructive if someone is capable of making you compromise in these areas.

Don't Ask For Permission

As children we are trained to constantly ask for permission, if we want to a drink, to eat, to go out to play. In school we had to ask permission to use the bathroom, we had to eat lunch at a certain time, wait in line to use the library. As a result people never stop waiting for permission to do things. Employees worldwide wait for a promotion, in a meeting they wait for their turn to speak, or even raise their hand which is a way of asking for permission.

Now that you are an adult, you should be able to do what you want to do when you want to do it. Your main concern should be with yourself and not with trying to satisfy the needs of everyone else around you. Manipulative people want you to feel as if there is an unspoken rule that does not allow you to make your own decisions that you have to get their permission for every decision that you make. You don't have to fall in line with this, simply do what you want to do when you want to do it.

Have a Sense of Purpose

People who are motivated by reaching their destiny are not easy to deceive. One of the main reasons why manipulators continue to succeed in the world is that there are too many people who live without a purpose. When you are not striving towards your destiny and determined to reach the goals that you have set for yourself, you fall in line with anything.

People who lack purpose, their days have no meaning and they float through life without any direction. They just go through the motions working in a job they don't like, watching reality TV, reading gossip magazines and wishing they lived someone else's life instead of working to become the best version of themselves. They keep busy with fruitless activities to fill the void of emptiness that grows within them day by day. This is what empowers manipulative people.

Manipulators control people with no purpose, and the only way to escape this fate is to find your destiny, when you are determined to make something of your life, you can't be distracted with the demands of someone who wants to control your life because you are the one who is in the driver's seat.

Expand Your Territories

The world wants you to play it safe and put all your eggs into one basket. Everything and everyone around you is telling you to lock yourself into the mundane routine of life, mortgage, car note, a boring but safe job, a boring but safe relationship and the list is endless. The world wants you to remain this way for the rest of your life, being ambitious is no longer admired and having a desire for the best is seen as a sign of weakness to those who are content with mediocrity. You will be accused of being greedy, and dissatisfied with life if you can't be content with the little that you have. When you express any desire to do and want more out of life, the manipulator will throw these accusations at you. They will call you arrogant, selfish, and prideful. They will attempt to make you feel uncomfortable with wanting to be successful in life.

The manipulator wants to keep you locked into the same position for the rest of your life. They want you to live in the same house, remain in the same relationship and stay in the same job so that you remain dependent upon them. When dealing with a manipulative person, the only way to stay independent is to create new opportunities, build new relationships, get a new job, start a new business and chase new experiences.

Stop Being a Punching Bag

If someone is able to fool you once, shame on them. If someone is able to fool you twice, shame on you! You need to have enough self respect and self awareness to say no to the person trying to manipulate you. The bottom line is that no one can manipulate you without your consent; you are responsible for everything that happens in your life. If anyone is capable of out-thinking or out-strategizing you, that's no one's fault but your own. You are going to have to learn from your mistakes, don't continue to trust the person that you know is trying to manipulate you.

Chapter 3: What is a Coward?

The coward of today isn't the person who is scared to walk into the haunted house, or the one who walks away from the fight, or the one who is afraid to stand up for themselves. Those days are over, there is now a new breed of coward, and if you evaluate their characteristics, they are actually pretty dangerous.

The modern day coward can be well dressed, and well spoken, he shows everyone that he can fit in to society and he makes sure that he hides his true character from the world.

The majority of people know at least one person who fits the description of a coward whether it's a family member, a friend or a work colleague but you just couldn't quite put your finger on how to label them. Here are the main signs of a modern day coward.

A Fear of Honesty

The modern day coward knows exactly who they are, and they realize that the real version of themselves can add nothing of value to anyone around them or society at large. Instead of taking the time to improve who they are they hide who they are and present a false image of themselves to the world. This image is typically one that says I am better than everyone else around them. They create an imaginary pedal stool and use it to elevate themselves above others. The modern coward is in complete denial and is comfortable living in their fake world.

They Avoid Strong People

A coward suffers from an extreme inferiority complex against a character who is resolute in their beliefs and knows exactly who they are. They don't like being in the presence of strong people because they know that a person with a strong mind has the ability to see straight through a weak person. The irony is that they harbor a secret admiration for strong people and really wish they could be like them. However, because they are so afraid of being exposed they hide from them.

They Only Associate With Weak People

The modern coward avoids strong people and they prey on the weak. They appear really nice and unthreatening to the weak person, but then their true colors are revealed as they start to do things like borrow money without paying it back. Or they are 35 years old and hanging out with 18 year olds because they know that the young mind is easy to manipulate.

They Manipulate People

The coward is a smooth operator, as we have learnt about manipulation everything they do has a motive behind it. A coward will look for your weaknesses so they can exploit you. This type of manipulation is actually an effective sales strategy, they will ask you probing and general questions so that they can find out how you think and behave. They will then use this information to evaluate your strengths and weaknesses and then use your weakness to gain an advantage over you.

A coward will bully you intellectually; this is another one of the reasons why they don't like to be around strong or intelligent people. They act as if they are experts in certain areas and take advantage of you by imposing alleged statistics, facts and other information that you might not have any knowledge about.

A coward will use aggressive manipulation by raising their voice during a conversation. The assumption is that if they project their voice loud enough, and feed you with negative emotions that you will submit to their needs and give them what they want. The aggressive voice is often combined with forceful body language such as excited gestures and standing up to intensify the situation.

They Never Admit They are in the Wrong

A coward is a coward because they are afraid, if they admit they are in the wrong they are scared that there will be a punishment attached to it. They are scared of showing people that they messed up because they want to appear as if they are perfect. In their mind there is no way they can be wrong because they have a false perception that they are superior to everyone and therefore they are always right.

They Don't Take Responsibility

A coward doesn't like to think about their weaknesses. In life when we make a mistake or do something wrong it is a reflection of our deficiencies. In general, no one likes to be reminded of their weaknesses and we most certainly don't want them exposed to other people. A coward doesn't want to face their weaknesses because it means that they will have to take responsibility for them and that is something they don't want to have to deal with.

They are Constantly Making Excuses

A reason and excuse are two totally different things. Things happen, if you are late because there was a car accident on the highway, that isn't your fault. However, if you were late because you woke up half an hour before your appointment but you are blaming your dad for being in the bathroom at the time you should have been at the reception desk signing in, that's an excuse.

A coward is always making excuses because they don't want to admit that they have failed or made a mistake. When they fail it was never their fault, it was out of their control. If they put on weight, it was because they were stressed out, if they lose their job it was because their boss had a vendetta against them, if his girlfriend dumps him, it's because she doesn't know what a real man is.

If the coward were to look at the reality of the situation and analyze where they went wrong they would find some simple truths. If they hadn't eaten burgers every day for six months they would never have put on weight. If they had come to work on time and worked hard they would have been seen as an asset to the team instead of a hindrance. If he had put more effort into his relationship, been more thoughtful, listened more, less selfish and less judgemental his girlfriend wouldn't have dumped him. A coward doesn't want to admit these things, they don't want to take responsibility for their actions and so they will make excuses and blame other people.

They are Conformists

A coward conforms to the status quo even though deep down they don't believe that it is right. For example, there are some men who are actually disgusted by the way society objectifies women through pornography. However, they will watch it when they are with a group of friends because everyone else is doing it. They are afraid to stand up and be counted because they don't want to be seen as different or they are afraid that people won't like them.

They Create Drama to Hide Their Mistakes

A coward creates drama in hopes that it will distract others from the mess they have made of a situation. They will break down and start crying uncontrollably for no reason so that people will feel sorry for them and be less harsh when the truth finally comes out.

They Never Follow Through

Have you ever seen anyone get into an argument and kick their chair to the side, stand up and don't throw a punch? By this time everyone has rushed around to calm the situation down. Then when their friends are in front of them they start leaning over and swearing and swinging their arms about! That's a coward! They don't follow through with anything all they do is talk about what they are going to do.

They are Bullies

Even though a coward is scared of just about anything, they are bullies. They feel like a failure, they are empty inside and instead of making things right in their life, they take their frustration out on other people.

They Look for Validation Online

A lot of cowards live on the internet through social media; it's a great way to hide who you really are. You can create an imaginary world where no one knows who you are and unless you are exposed as a fraud you can be as fake as silicone breasts and no one will ever know.

There is nothing wrong with being on social media if you are presenting the truth about yourself, but if you want to live a fairytale online life, there is defiantly something wrong with this.

They Don't Like Being Alone

When you don't like yourself very much you don't want to be alone. When you are alone it's difficult to drown out the voices in your head reminding you that you are a complete failure and so you are constantly seeking validation from people. However, even though a coward doesn't like being alone, they can't be around anyone as mentioned earlier, they don't like being around strong people because they can't fool them. They have to be around people that make them feel superior, people who will praise them and people who are not going to see through the mask that they are wearing.

Passive Aggressive

A coward will never say what they really mean. Do you have a friend that is constantly updating their facebook profile with ridiculous statements that are clearly directed at you but they will never say so openly. For example, you are unable to attend their dinner party because you have to study for an exam and within an hour of you telling them this they change their status to "real friends are supportive."

In other words they are too scared to speak their mind, and they know that you know they are talking about you but if you confront them you know they are going to deny it so you don't bother. In this way they think they have control over you. A coward is also an attention seeker and doing things like constantly changing the status on their facebook page with these indirect comments is a way for them to get the attention that they want. When people start sending messages about why they have changed their status they will spend hours telling everyone else about the problem but won't tell the person they are directing their comments to.

They Get in Arguments to Cover up Their Flaws

Have you ever got in an argument with someone who starts insulting you and pointing out your weak areas to divert from the main point which is that they have made a complete mess of things?

When you try and get them to see things from your point of view, they respond with, "SO WHAT?" Do you remember when you......." And they will bring up a mistake from the past that has absolutely nothing to do with what has just transpired.

They Don't Believe They Can Make Things Right

It can be hard to face reality, especially when you have made such a mess of things that you think no one will ever forgive you or believe that you are capable of changing your life. They also find it difficult to forgive themselves.

With the coward everything boils down to fear and so they just carry on walking down that same path of self destruction.

Chapter 4: How to Deal With a Coward

As you have read a coward has several different character traits therefore you will need to incorporate several different methods to handle them. Here are some ideas:

Don't bite the bait

There is a fine line between responding to a coward and taking part in the drama they are creating. Cowards love attention, and they will purposely do little annoying things just to get a reaction out of you. So you should avoid asking questions such as: "What did you mean by that? Or Why did you make that comment?

Example: If the coward says "thank you" but sounds and looks like he is angry, answer in content and not in the context of the situation. So your response should be "you are welcome!" Because what they are expecting you to say is "why did you say it like that?" In this way you are meeting the person where they are without falling into their trap. A coward wants to watch you squirm and rack your brains trying to figure out what's wrong with them. If you don't give them what they want, it disarms them.

Talk About Today

There are times when a coward is going to aggravate you so much that you just have to pull them to the side for five minutes and give them a piece of your mind. There is a high possibility that this is not the first time they have behaved this way; however, when you are speaking to them make sure you stick to what happened on that day without bringing up the past. Bringing up old emotions is pointless, plus it actually gives the person power over you. When someone knows that they have the ability to get under your skin they are going to keep pushing your buttons.

Example: Your friend says, "Those pants look great on you, they really hide your extra weight." Cowards like to give back handed insults. Even though your blood is going to be boiling at this time, don't respond in anger and go on about how she is always criticizing you. Instead, focus on that moment and let her know how you feel at that time.

Speak with Authority

Cowards like to try and manipulate people, the best way to avoid falling victim to this is if you are assertive. This means that any time you speak to them do so with authority, never sound as if you are uncertain or indecisive or they will jump on you.

Example: Your friend has invited you to a dinner party at his house. You have told him you don't want any alcohol but while he is pouring you an orange juice you see him pouring in a drop of vodka. You know why you don't want to have any alcohol on that that night, so at this point you have to approach him and firmly say: "I watched you pour vodka in my orange juice, now I told you that I don't want any alcohol and that's final!" You don't need to explain yourself, its none of his business, but there are times when you are going to have to put your foot down.

Consequences for Their Actions

Cowards create a lot of drama; another way to get them to change their behavior is to ensure that there are direct consequences for their actions. Assess how their behavior has had a negative effect on you and then decide on your response.

Example: You have been to the movies three times this month and this is the third time they have been late. They don't call, text, when you call their phone just rings out and when they get there they have some elaborate excuse for being late! Let them know that if this happens one more time you will not be inviting them out to the movies again!

The bottom line is that a coward has underlying psychological problems and as annoying as they can be what you are dealing with is a broken person. I am a firm believer in compassion because we all have broken places in our lives it's just that some people are better at managing it than others. Make sure that you take this into consideration when you are dealing with a coward in your life.

Chapter 5: Dealing With a Liar

It is essential that you learn to master your emotional reaction when handling a liar. You are not responsible for changing their behavior but you are responsible for changing the way you react towards them. One important point to remember first of all is that everyone lies to some degree. Technically a lie is a lie, we have all heard the term a white lie which involves telling a small lie here and there and then there are people who lie continuously for no reason, these people are referred to as pathological and compulsive liars.

Change Starts With Awareness

One of the most interesting facts about lying is that the way we are socially conditioned actually trains us to lie. In many social situations it is actually required of us. When you can understand how people are socialized, your expectations are going to be different. This does not mean that you should condone lying; it simply means that you don't take it as an offense, or you don't take it to heart. This awareness enables you to deal with the situation without reacting to it emotionally.

How we are Trained to Lie

We are trained to lie so that we don't appear rude. Do you not remember your mother telling you to say the food of a friend or a relative was delicious even if you hated it? This is lying to be respectful so that you don't hurt anyone's feelings. You might have thrown the food under the table to the cat, when the host asks, "How was your meal?" You respond by saying, "Oh it was delicious."

If your granny asks you if you like her pink fluffy hat, you are going to say yes even though you can't stand it and your parents are not going to chastise you for sparing granny's feelings. The funny thing is that if you had said that you think it's awful and granny starts crying, you would probably get into trouble. This is how we are trained to lie and it slowly becomes a normal part of our existence.

We lie to avoid punishment

If you went to a friend's house after school to play and one of your main activities was to climb on to the roof of the garage and jump down onto the grass but you know that is something you have been told not to do. When you go home and your parents ask you what you got up to, you are going to leave that part out so that you don't incriminate yourself.

We Lie to Build Loyalty and Trust

I am going to use myself as an example here. When I was a child and I was playing with my friends in the house, if we broke a household item that we were not supposed to be playing with we would make a pact that we would say we don't know what happened to it. When our parents would ask who broke the item, we would all say the same thing, "I don't know!" This turns the desire to be loyal to each other into a lie, our parents are not stupid and they know that we are lying so this then defeats the purpose. In our quest for trust and loyalty, our parents end up not trusting us because we have lied.

Lying to Authority Figures

Lying to our parents, teaches us to lie to other people of authority later on in life. When we are settled into our careers and upper management decides to introduce a new policy into the company that you don't agree with, do you tell them this? No! You remain quiet because you do not want to create conflict with the people who have your livelihood in their hands. Even when they ask you to assist them in the decision making process, it is easier to go with the status quo. We then discuss our concerns with work colleagues that are on the same level as us and have no power to fire us if they don't like our opinion.

You may have a great relationship with your manager where you are able to speak with them freely about the things that are taking place within the company. However, you would not have the same conversation with the CEO! The majority of employees don't, giving your honest opinion is the equivalent to putting a noose around your own neck if what you have to say doesn't line up with the opinions of upper management.

A Liar Does Not Want to Offend People

In a personal relationship we lie so that we don't offend the people that we care about. If a couple are in a strictly monogamous relationship and the woman starts to have feelings for her boss at work, she is not going to run home and tell her partner. Even if her partner suspects the affair, she is not going to admit it when he asks.

If a survey was taken asking if there was anything wrong with this type of lying the majority of people would chalk it up to harmless "white lies." However, when bigger lies are told, the motivations are the same. When a man is having an affair, unless he is planning on getting a divorce he is not going to tell his wife. The affair was something that just happened but he still wants to keep his marriage intact; therefore, every time he is late home from work from seeing the other woman, he is going to lie about it. If your friend was playing around on her husband and he asked you because he suspected would you tell him? The majority of people wouldn't.

We Lie When we Don't Want to Involve Anyone in Our Problems

If someone hurts our feelings and we are asked about it, we lie and say it's not an issue when deep down we are devastated and our blood is boiling. This is also a form of emotional denial, we tell others we are not upset or offended so that we don't have to confront the fact that we are upset.

Chapter 6: Pathological Lying

Pathological lying is also referred to as mythomania and pseudologia fantastica. The term was coined by psychologist Anton Delbruek in 1891. Pathological lying is defined as a complete distortion of the truth. The individual is either conscious of the lies they are telling or they actually believe that they are telling the truth. The characteristics of a pathological liar include:

They Suffer From a Mental Disorder or a Personality Disorder

Pathological lying has not been classified as a mental illness, but it is often one of the characteristics of a mental condition. Pathological lying is a common symptom of narcissistic personality disorder and borderline personality disorder. If you know anyone who has been diagnosed with a mental illness they may also be a pathological liar.

Attention Seekers

Therapist Mark Tyrell suggests that pathological liars do so to get attention. People who want to be the center of attention wherever they are may invent stories so that people will be interested in what they have to say. They love having an audience present and they get an adrenaline rush from the response that they get which leads them to lie even more. If you know anyone who is always seeking attention, there is a high possibility that a lot of what they say is a lie.

They Lie to Make Themselves or Their Situation Look Better

A pathological liar finds it hard to admit that they are struggling. They want everyone to believe that they are living this perfect life. Instead they will either only discuss the good times, or they will create stories to make the bad times look good.

They Are Always Playing the Victim Role

Playing the victim is another way for them to gain attention. They want to influence and control the thoughts, feelings and actions of others. They play the victim role as a coping mechanism so that they don't have to face the reality that they are in the situation that they are in because of the choices they have made. The pathological liar plays this role in order to draw out the nurturing, caring and protective qualities in other people; they then use this as a way of manipulating others.

When pathological liars play the victim role, they don't seem to learn from their mistakes because they are always walking into the same problems. For example they are constantly having the same relationship issues, they speak to a friend about it who gives them wise advice only to find that the same problem is still there in a month's time and they are crying on the phone again telling the same story.

The pathological liar plays the victim role through their constant complaints, they always have some drama going on in their life and they poison other people with their negativity.

They play the victim role by bragging indirectly. For example, they will say things like "I am so tired, my girlfriend wouldn't let me sleep." In other words "I am so good in bed that my girlfriend couldn't get enough of me." This is a very aggressive manipulation tactic and an ego boosting method administered by their imagined superiority to others. When people humble brag, they are indirectly trying to tell you that they are better than you.

If you know anyone who is always sick with different illnesses, or something bad is always happening to them you can be pretty certain that person is a pathological liar.

Low Self Esteem

The majority of behavioral issues are related to low self esteem. People with low self esteem are more likely be pathological liars because they want others to think that they are better than they know that they are.

Chapter 7: Compulsive Lying

Compulsive lying and pathological lying are similar but they are not the same and the two are often confused. A pathological liar lies to manipulate people and get what they want without any regard for the feelings of others. On the other hand, they are both associated with antipersonality disorder. Despite the fact that it is not documented in the Manual of Mental Disorders, the majority of psychologists and psychiatrists consider it to be a mental disorder.

Over the last two decades there has been an extensive amount of research conducted on compulsive lying. However, it is still one of the most under researched psychiatric illnesses.

Individuals suffering from this disorder are simply unable to control their desire to lie. They get so caught up in the stories that they tell that they believe in their own lies. Even when it is discovered that they are lying and they are confronted, they will be adamant that they are telling the truth and will even attempt to get others to back them up who know nothing about the story that they are telling. They end up confusing you because they are so convincing in their denial.

Practice makes perfect, and the more they practice lying the easier it becomes for them to convince others that they are telling the truth. There are a limited amount of statistics detailing how many people suffer from compulsive lying disorder, but it is just as common in men as it is women and symptoms begin to surface in the late teens. There are several defining characteristics associated with compulsive lying disorder:

- Their stories are not completely unbelievable, and they often contain an element of truth. Their lies are not a result of delusions or some other type of psychosis.
- The tendency to fabricate stories is rarely due to social pressure or their immediate

circumstances but it is an unfortunate personality trait in the individual. For example, they will lie with no logical explanation when asked a simple question such as "what is your favorite meal?"

- The motive for lying is internal and not external and the individual will require a clinical assessment to determine what they are.

- Compulsive lying disorder typically develops during childhood. It stems from the child's need to seek attention from peers and caregivers. While making up stories during childhood people were either fascinated or disgusted by their lies. Either way they gained the much needed attention from the people they were entertaining. Parents are well aware that children can engage their imaginations with stories, and so parents will often allow their kids to get away with lying assuming that it is an innocent childhood phase and they will grow out of it.

However, when the lies are allowed to continue, it can develop into compulsive lying disorder.

- Compulsive liars always want to feel as if they are superior to others and that they deserve more attention than anybody else. To achieve this goal, they will make up grandiose stories about themselves that portrays them as the hero in the eyes of those who are listening.

- A compulsive liar will take extreme precautions to ensure that his deception is not discovered. Every so often, a web of lies will get unraveled and the liar is exposed. When this happens the liar will work quickly to rebuild the wall of deception that was once erected. This typically involves telling more lies which typically involves them being the victim of a false accusation.

- A compulsive liar will take interesting stories they have heard from friends or family and make themselves the main character.

- The stories tend to present the individual in a favorable light. For example they might tell a lie that focuses on how brave they are, or that they are connected to several famous people.

There are currently several theories that explain why an individual might develop compulsive lying disorder. Some research indicates that it is due to a neurological imbalance in the frontal lobe. The British Journal of Psychiatry published a study that discovered that pathological liars have an excessive concentration of white matter in the brain which predisposes them to the condition.

Several psychologists and psychiatrists believe that people with low self esteem who are consciously or unconsciously looking for popularity, attention, love or attempting to cover up for their failures in life are susceptible to developing this disorder. Finally, there are theories that compulsive lying is a response to childhood neglect or trauma. Or the parents failure to establish boundaries, limits and guidance during childhood.

Due to compulsive lying disorder not being a recognized mental disorder, there is no diagnostic criteria for the condition. However, many psychologists and psychiatrists will diagnose a person based on the behavioral patterns reported by family members and friends. There is no direct cure for the condition, the only viable solution is therapy; however, therapy is only effective if the individual wants to get help. If the compulsive liar is in denial that they have a problem, they are not going to want to seek help.

If therapy is administered, it will be aimed at treating the addictive element of the disorder as well as teaching the individual how their lies have a negative effect on those around them. They will also receive assistance in changing disruptive thinking patterns. If there are underlying issues with low self esteem and depression, some psychiatrists might prescribe anti-depressants.

Chapter 8: How to Detect When a Person is Lying

Susan Carnicero, Philip Houston, and Michael Floyd are all former CIA officers. Together they wrote a book entitled "Spy the Lie" which provides detailed professional information about how to tell when someone is lying. The authors make reference to several signs that will let you know when someone is not telling the truth, here is the condensed version.

Behavioral Delay or Pause: Typically, when you ask a person a question there is a few seconds delay while the question is contemplated before it is answered. The length of the delay is important in determining whether or not the person is telling the truth. This depends on the type of question the person is asked. Here is an example:

If you ask a friend a random question such as "What were you doing on Monday April 17th seven years ago?" Your friend is naturally going to pause for a number of reasons. First, it is not a normal question, the person will have to think about it and most people won't be able to give an adequate answer because they simply can't remember that far back. If you ask your friend, "Did you rob a bank on Monday April 17th 7 years ago?" If they pause before responding you might need to consider whether this is someone you want to maintain a friendship with because this is a question that there should not be any pause and your friend should immediately respond with a sharp "No!" This is a simple exercise that helps you to understand that the delay in response should be relative to the type of question being asked.

Verbal and Non Verbal Mismatch: Our brains have been created in such a way that when we speak our body language says the same thing that is coming out of our mouth. When the body is saying something different to what is being said, deception is taking place.

Examples include a person nodding their head to affirm themselves, but they are saying "No." On the flip side, shakes their head to say "No," but they are saying yes. Due to the fact that it is so natural for the verbal and the non verbal to mirror each other, you would find it very difficult to do as an exercise. However, those who lie on a regular basis do so without thinking about it.

There are some points to consider when applying this principle. First, it only applies when an extensive response is required and not if they reply with a short sentence or a one word answer. For example, a person might nod sharply when saying "No!" This is not considered a body language contradiction but a way of emphasizing the point. Second, it depends on who you are speaking to and what country they are from because in some cultures "yes" is not indicated with nodding and "no" is not indicated with shaking the head.

Hide the Eyes or Mouth: A person who is not telling the truth will often shield their eyes or mouth. It is natural to want to hide the fact that you are lying; therefore, if a person puts their hand over their mouth when answering a question, it indicates deception. If a person hides their eyes, it may be a subconscious way of hiding from the reaction of the lie they have just told. The person might close their eyes or put their hand over their eyes, both of which are indicators of deception.

Swallowing or Clearing the Throat: If a person swallows hard or clears their throat before answering the question, they are probably lying. If this takes place after they have given the answer, this is not a problem; you should only get suspicious if they do so beforehand. Two things might be taking place when swallowing or clearing the throat. They are either dressing up their lie in their head before saying it in a "I swear to God...." Or the question might have caused them to become anxious and uncomfortable which can manifest with a dry mouth.

Hand or Face Activity: You should be weary of a person who bites or licks their lips, or pulls on their ears or lips. The individual becomes nervous or anxious about the question being asked because they would incriminate themselves if they spoke the truth. This causes the nervous system to go into action causing the blood to drain from the surface of the ears or face which creates an itching or cold sensation. The hands are then unconsciously drawn to those areas. Another indicator that a person is lying is rubbing or wringing of the hands.

Grooming Gestures: A person attempting to conceal the truth will often begin to groom themselves or their surrounding area. For example, a man might adjust his shirt cuffs; a woman might straighten her skirt or smooth her hair over. If a person starts sweating and they pull out a handkerchief and wipes their brow when responding to the question you are possibly dealing with a liar.

Another type of grooming is tidying up their surroundings. When a question is asked all of a sudden the pencil is out of place, or the magazines on the desk need straightening, or there is some dust on the windowsill. They are indirectly trying to divert your attention from the lies that they are telling.

Blinking: Lying requires that a person concentrates more than they usually would. Research has discovered that people don't blink as much when they are in deep concentration. For example there will be a difference in blinking habits when trying to remember an 8 digit number as opposed to a four digit number. In experiments where one group of participants were asked to lie about something and others were not, the liars didn't blink as much. However, blinking is also dependent upon the reason for the lie and how you feel about the need to lie. When a person is lying about something they have done wrong and they feel anxious about it, they are likely to blink more.

Dilated Pupils: This is another indication of concentration and tension. The pupils of the liar might dilate when they are concentrating or feeling tense and anxious. However, even with an obvious sign like this, there is also a possibility of "false positives," people can become extremely anxious and over think the details to a question being asked even when they are innocent.

Micro Facial Expressions: A study conducted by Paul Ekman, a facial expressions and lying expert found that the key to determine whether or not a person is lying is through micro facial expressions. They are expressions that come and go on a person's face so quickly that unless you were paying close attention you will not notice them. During research to compile a list of everyday facial expressions, Ekman examined a series of video tapes and found that there were some facial expressions that lasted a 20th of a second. These fleeting expressions reveal the true motives that we are trying so hard to disguise.

Ekman uses the example of a woman accused of murdering her husband and her facial expressions during police interrogation. She may appear as if she is eager to cooperate with the police, but a particular question causes her to flash a micro-expression of anger. What is the reason behind that expression of anger? Is she angry because the question has exposed a lie? If she hasn't been asked a question, and no comments have been made, what does a brief smile indicate? Could it be a smile of triumph?

If you suspect that someone is lying to you, have a conversation with them and watch out for any of the signs that have been mentioned.

Chapter 9: How to Deal With a Liar

Lying is not an attractive quality, but regardless of how people act there is always a right way and a wrong way to treat them. If you know someone in your life who is a pathological or a compulsive liar it can be difficult not to lose your temper with them especially at the moment that the lie is being released from their mouth and you are fully aware that what they are telling you is not the truth. Here are some methods to assist you in dealing with a liar.

Keep Your Guard up.

Prepare yourself mentally knowing that you cannot accept or trust what this person is saying. You should always expect the outcome of a situation to be different than anticipated because of the nature of the person you are dealing with.

If the liar is someone you are close to it can be difficult because it is easy to get your hopes up and decide that this time you are going to give them the benefit of the doubt. It is almost as if you are in denial concerning the fact that this individual lies the way they do. Unless you want to get hurt, you can't afford to do this, you need to have your guard up constantly.

Make Records of Conversations

This isn't something that you really want to do in your spare time; however, documenting things that have been said can be very helpful. A liar will attempt to convince you that they didn't say what you are quoting, that you are exaggerating or that you indeed are the one who is lying. They can be so convincing that you either decide that you heard wrong or that you are going crazy! Unless it is something really serious, or you are in a relationship with this person and they have agreed to get therapy, you don't need to present the documented notes because it can do more harm than good.

Don't Focus on the Lies

If you want to know how to deal with a liar, you must care for the individual and still want them in your life or you would just walk away and forget about it. If you still want this person in your life they must have some good qualities and this is what you should focus on. If you keep your attention on the lies they tell, you will find yourself becoming increasingly angry and bitter towards the person which in the end is only hurting yourself.

Ignore Their Stories

When the liar in your life starts to tell you one of their fables, don't feed into it. A liar will often tell stories for attention, when you don't give it to them they will stop. Society tells us to treat everyone with kindness and respect what a person has to say. However, when the person speaking is breaking all the rules, you can do the same. The liar will probably ask you why you are being so nonchalant towards them, be honest and let them know that you don't want to be the one to encourage them to continue lying. You won't know how the individual is going to react to this comment. They will either try and convince you that they are telling the truth, admit that they are lying or not say anything and start thinking about the damage that their lies are doing to your relationship.

Be Patient

If you want to maintain a friendship/romantic relationship/workplace acquaintance with this individual you are going to have to be patient with them. The bottom line is that this individual has a problem and they need help. Everyone has their own demons to fight, theirs just happens to affect everyone else around them. If you want to relieve some of the frustration of having to deal with a person that you can't trust you might want to speak to a mutual friend who understands what is going on. You can put your heads together to try and confront the issue constructively.

Pick Your Battles

Liars tell so many tales that if you call out every untruth you are going to wear yourself out emotionally. Therefore, pick your battles wisely. Maybe you can ignore the small lies but confront the big stories or the lies that do damage to the credibility of others.

Don't be Argumentative When Confronting Them

When you decide to confront the liar don't get confrontational. If you don't want the person to get defensive and retreat into their shell, you are going to have to be very tactile in your approach towards them. It wouldn't be a good idea to start your conversation with: "You are a sorry liar!" Instead you should give the liar the opportunity to correct their lie. For example, if you find out that your boyfriend said that he was going to help his mother paint the house in the afternoon but he didn't go, instead of saying: "I spoke to your mom earlier." Start the conversation with, "So how did it go at your mom's today?" Allow them to respond, and if they continue the lie by saying, "Oh, it went really well, the house looks fantastic, we went to IKEA and picked a great color...." You can then say, "Your mom called me today and said that you didn't come around, why are you lying?

Disrupt Their Habit of Lying

The first time that you do this is going to be really awkward, but it will get easier as time goes on. When you catch them out in a lie let them know that what they have said is not the truth, but don't say so in a judgemental way. Your aim is to get them to realize that they are not fooling anyone with their lies and that it would be in their best interest to speak the truth at all times. Since lying is habitual, you are going to have to call them out on their lies several times before the message starts to register.

Be Tactful

You need to let the individual know that you are aware of their lies without being too direct about it. So the next time they come up with one of their elaborate stories such as "I was once the hairdresser for the queen of England," you can say something witty like, "Oh, like how you shaved Britney Spears head? Remember you telling me that?" They will probably attempt to convince you that they are telling the truth, you don't need to get irate simply smile and stay calm but let them know in no uncertain terms that their history of storytelling speaks for itself.

You are not holding a grudge against them or trying to make them feel small. The aim here is to let them know that their history of lying is making it very difficult for you to believe what they tell you.

Suggest That They Get Help

As with all solutions that involve confrontation, this can be very sensitive. Suggesting that they get help could backfire because therapy is for people who want to get help. If they are not willing to admit that they have a problem, they are going to get offended when you suggest therapy. If you have had counseling or you know someone who has, you can start by mentioning how well it helped in overcoming the problem.

Chapter 10: Dealing with Thieves

A 20 year Pinkerton study discovered that 30 percent of the American population would steal whenever the opportunity presented itself. Forty percent will steal if they know they will definitely get away with it and not face any consequences, and a mere 30 percent said that they would never steal. But I would say confidently that even though the 30 percent wouldn't steal, they would definitely be tempted especially if:

- They would get away with it
- If what they were stealing was something they really needed
- If it was a small item that wouldn't be missed
- If you feel that there will be no financial burden on the government agency or the company being stolen from

People don't need a lot of encouragement to steal. According to a National Retail and Security

Survey, missing inventory from a combination of shoplifting and employee theft costs U.S. retailers more than $31 billion a year which is 1.7 percent of their total annual sales. In the retail industry, this phenomenon is referred to as "inventory shrinkage," it is the largest category of larceny in the U.S.A, more than bank robbery, motor vehicle theft and home burglary combine! This type of theft hurts consumers the most because prices go up to cover the costs of their losses. The average family will spend over $440 per year in price increases because of inventory theft.

The internet has opened up a whole new world for thieves and this typically comes in the form of identity theft. USA Today reported that identity theft costs individuals $5 billion a year in out of pocket expenses and almost $48 billion a year in losses to financial institutions and businesses.

The majority of people are not aware of this but there are different categories of thieves. Most of us just assume that a thief is lazy and can't be bothered to get a job or that they have an addiction problem. You will be surprised to know that there is more to stealing than just stealing!

Chapter 11: Atypical Theft Behavior

According to the DSM, atypical theft offending (ATO) is not a diagnosable condition. Despite the fact that it has not been registered as a universal condition does not mean that it doesn't exist. Dr Will Cupchik has spent forty years studying the condition as well as providing treatment for sufferers. He defines an ATO as "A person who does not steal out of necessity or greed but as a behavioral response to issues that have not been dealt with subconsciously. Often the items that are stolen have a symbolic meaning."

ATO is a psychological disorder in which shoplifting or stealing becomes a coping mechanism for the sufferer. ATO's generally have very low self esteem regardless of how successful they are in life. The condition begins to manifest during the late teenage years or early adulthood, although there have been cases where the elderly and children have also suffered from the condition.

Cupchik suggested several reasons for atypical theft behavior, these include:

- A loss of a relationship
- The loss of a job
- Sickness, e.g. being diagnosed with a life threatening condition such as cancer
- An unconscious desire for retribution
- The unconscious desire to manipulate

Cupchik suggested that suffers steal as a way of subconsciously compensating for their loss.

An American lawyer earning more than $800,000 per year went to see a psychiatrist about her stealing habits. She had been through a very traumatic pregnancy where she was told that there was a high possibility that the baby will not survive and if the baby did survive it would be severely disabled with many life threatening problems. Fortunately the child was born successfully, but it had a minor physical defect of a very small big toe on its right foot. After her baby was born, whenever any of her friends gave birth she would buy them elaborate toys or clothing and at the same time steal something small from the store she was making her purchase. From what she can remember, she has stolen on more than twenty separate occasions, but the habit only started after the birth of her child. The items she stole were typically less than $20, and considering the profession that she was in, if she was ever caught and found guilty she would not only risk losing her job but also the chance to ever practice law again.

She decided to seek psychiatric help after she was approached by an employee after he witnessed her put an item into her bag. While she managed to talk herself out of him calling the police by claiming that it was an absent minded act and she accidently put the item in her bag while searching for her credit card. The experience scared her into seeking help for her behavior because next time she might not be so lucky.

During her therapy sessions, it was discovered that her parents were extremely oppressive and expected her to be the perfect child at all times. She then had to deal with giving birth to a child who was not perfect; even though it only had a minor defect it affected her psychologically as the painful memories of her quest for perfection during childhood were brought back to life through her son.

Each time she thought of buying a present for her friend's baby she felt guilty, envious and frustrated that she had failed in the pursuit of perfection in her own children.

A man by the name of Victor, a retired business owner and Holocaust survivor was apprehended after stealing $15 worth of goods from a store in Los Angeles. As is the case of all Holocaust survivors, Victor had overcome terror and tragedy, despite of what he went through he succeeded in becoming successful in his personal and career life. In spite of his success, there was always that underlying, lingering sadness and horror of what he had been through.

All of Victor's family members which included his parents, four grandparents and four siblings had been killed in Nazi concentration camps. During his therapy, he remembered with deep emotion as his family had been herded off like cattle to the slaughter. His friend pulled him back from joining the line with his family and told him to "look strong and stand up straight," so that the German soldiers would think that he would be of benefit to them. His life was spared because the German soldiers believed him to be healthy and strong and he ended up working for them. When the war ended Victor migrated to America and started a new life.

Victor was a hard worker; he eventually built his own successful business, married and had three children. Due to the horrific nature in which he lost his family members, he decided to live a morally upstanding life as a way of honoring them. When he went against his own code of conduct and was caught shop lifting from a Los Angeles store, he was more shocked than anyone else. Victor was later referred to a psychiatrist.

Victor was a senior citizen when he started stealing; when he was interviewed by the psychiatrist he was unable to explain his behavior. All he could remember was that he walked into a drugstore, picked up an item, put it in his coat pocket and attempted to walk out of the store. When he talked about his time at the concentration camp, he described in detail the night that he was set free. All of the prisoners were told to wake up in the middle of the night; they were marched out of the camp in the dark. They believed that they were being taken out to die like they had witnessed happen to thousands before them, maybe shot to death in the woods and then buried in a grave that had been prepared for them.

Victor remembered that no one was wearing shoes or socks as they walked across a rocky rail line. He recalled that his feet were deeply cut and bruised and he struggled to walk. He said that they were forced to walk for more than three hours; any of the prisoners who fell and found it difficult to get up were shot immediately. Despite the pain, Victor chose to stay on his feet and keep moving as fast as he could.

He went on to state that after those terrifying hours of staggering along the rail line, they were informed that the war was over and they were free to go. The German soldiers let them know that the Allied soldiers and the Red Cross were on their way so they should stay where they were. The soldiers then ran away, when the Red Cross trucks arrived the prisoners were attended to and their injured feet were wrapped in bandages and salve.

Victor was set free on April 12, 1945; on April 12, 1995 he walked into a drugstore and stole a packet of Dr Scholl's insoles when he didn't have any need for the product. When he realized the connection he began to cry. After a few emotional moments Victor said "I stole the insoles for my feet that were hurting in 1945."

Victor later mentioned that since his arrival in America, he always made sure that he had more than enough footwear. He purchased the most expensive shoes and always ensured that they were kept in the best condition. He also realized that the day that he stole was the fiftieth anniversary of the day that he was set free. He said that he never discussed his experience with family or friends; he simply got on with his life as if the tragedy never occurred.

Even though Victor attempted to block the event from his conscious mind, his unconscious mind recognized the date as the 50th anniversary of his freedom which is what lead to him stealing.

During 1995, America and the rest of the world celebrated the end of World War II and especially the end of the Holocaust. Victor avoided any connection to these proceedings because he did not want to be reminded of what he had been through.

Most readers will agree that Victor's act of theft does not warrant judgement but compassion.

While the majority of atypical theft behavior doesn't have the same dramatic story as Victor's as a justification, there are very similar psychodynamics among them. Many of those involved in this type of theft after receiving therapy it has become clear that their unconscious minds have been reminded of painful and traumatic memories.

Here are some other examples of theft that could be labeled as atypical:

In 2002, it became worldwide headline news that famous actress Winona Ryder had been caught walking out of Saks in Beverly Hills with over $4000 worth of goods.

In 2003, another famous actress Shelley Morrison from the sitcom Will & Grace was caught stealing from a store.

In 2012, Mary Hayashi, the wife of an Alameda County Superior court judge was apprehended after leaving a Neimnan Marcus store without paying for $2,500 worth of clothing. She was charged with misdemeanor shoplifting and pleaded no contest. She was fined less than $200 and sentenced to three years probation.

In 2007, Henry Sobel one of Brazil's most prominent and well respected rabbis who is recognized worldwide for his courage and unblemished reputation was arrested for stealing neckties in Palm Beach, Florida.

In 2006, President George W. Bush's Domestic Policy advisor Claude Allen also a lawyer resigned from his position after being caught attempting to defraud Target of an expensive stereo. He purchased the item, went and left it in his car and then returned to the store picked up the same stereo, took it to the cash desk and asked for a refund using the receipt for the stereo that was in his car.

In 1993, John W. Shannon, the Acting Secretary of the United States army was caught stealing a mere $30 worth of items.

Hedy Lamarr is not only an actress but also holds a U.S patent was arrested in 1991 for stealing laxative and eye drops from a pharmacy in Florida. She had also been arrested in 1966 for stealing in Los Angeles.

In 1988, Bess Myerson the New York City Cultural Affairs Commissioner and former Miss America stole less than $50 worth of goods from a store.

A long standing state police officer walked into a department store and stole two pairs of gloves in front of a hidden surveillance camera that he was aware of because he had previously been called to the store to arrest people for stealing. He had sat and watched footage from the same camera that recorded him stealing.

A well known surgeon was apprehended after he was caught stealing cash and jewelry from other surgeons while they were in the operating room.

A public school teacher known for winning several awards for her service was caught stealing from several stores including clothing stores and supermarkets.

Chapter 12: Kleptomania

What is Kleptomania?

Kleptomania is a psychiatric condition where the sufferer feels an uncontrollable urge to steal something. Once the theft has taken place, this urge is released until it comes upon them again. Kleptomania has been labeled as an impulse control disorder, but it also falls under the umbrella of obsessive-compulsive disorder.

A person who suffers from kleptomania is referred to as a kleptomaniac and will typically suffer from another psychiatric disorder such as an anxiety or eating disorder. They may also have a drug or alcohol addiction. According to the Diagnostic and Statistical Manual of Mental Disorders kleptomania is characterized by the following symptoms:

- The inability to refrain from stealing things that they do not need, neither do they have any economic value.

- A heightened sense of physical pressure prior to the act of theft being performed.

- A sense of fulfillment and satisfaction once the act of theft has been carried out.

- Theft is not carried out because of revenge or to antagonize anyone. Neither is it a reaction to a fantasy or a delusion.

- Theft is not due to a behavior disorder, antisocial personality disorder or a manic episode.

The inability to stop stealing leads to a destructive mental condition that prevents the person from living a productive life. There is a great deal of guilt and shame associated with kleptomania as well as the risk of severe legal consequences. This is a debilitating mood disorder that has a negative effect on the individual, family, friends and loved ones.

Kleptomania Statistics

There have not been many studies conducted on kleptomania; therefore, statistics are scarce. However, the condition is more common than originally thought. The typical kleptomaniac is a thirty five year old woman who started stealing at the age of twenty, stealing brings a combination of guilt and relief.

- It is estimated that there are approximately 1.2 million kleptomaniacs in the United States.
- Kleptomania accounts for an estimated 5% of all shoplifting
- Kleptomania typically starts in the late teenage years or early adulthood and it appears to be more common in women than in men.

The Causes of Kleptomania

There are currently no known causes as to why a person develops kleptomania. Some psychologists believe that it is connected to drug and alcohol addiction. Others believe that it is a form of impulse control such as obsessive compulsive disorder or eating disorders. In the most cases, the individual does not only suffer from kleptomania but with another psychiatric condition.

Symptoms of Kleptomania

Symptoms of kleptomania are often wrongly diagnosed as common theft, but there are several symptoms associated with kleptomania, these include:

- A powerful desire to steal items that are not a necessity
- Invasive thoughts
- Incapable of resisting the urge to steal
- A feeling of relief after the theft
- Remorse
- Stress

Effects of Kleptomania

Kleptomaniacs suffer a lot of emotional pain, it is not possible to cure the disease it can only be managed. Kleptomaniacs find it difficult to live a normal life, emotional effects include the following:

- Guilt
- Stress
- Shame
- Remorse
- Battling with another type of mood disorder

The physical effects of kleptomania are pretty obvious:

- Arrest
- Incarceration

There are also several unwanted social consequences associated with kleptomania:

- Labeled as a thief
- People are unable to trust you
- Isolated from loved ones

- Criminal record

Treatment For Kleptomania

The individual living with kleptomania disorder has to live with strong feelings of shame, guilt and remorse. If the disorder is left untreated, the person has to deal with these feelings continuously. There is currently no cure for the condition; however, the best way to manage kleptomania is through a combination of behavioral and pharmaceutical treatments. Professional help is available from licensed therapists through a kleptomania treatment center.

Chapter 13: How to Handle a Thief

My hope is that after reading the preceding chapter, you understand that there are some people who don't steal because they are too lazy to get job and buy the things that they want. Just like every other abnormal human trait, as you have read, the habit of stealing is easily explained once you have a good understanding of the person's history, unmet needs and childhood experiences. If you have a close relationship with someone who steals before you lose your temper and do something you will regret or pick up the phone and dial 911, you need to get a better understanding of what is driving them psychologically so that you can try and help them.

You Know Your Friend is a Thief But You Don't Have Direct Evidence

You don't want to believe that your friend is a thief but every time they are around things keep on going missing. So what do you do? This is a touchy subject because you can't accuse people of stealing based on a hunch. It would be better if you had concrete evidence but since you don't you are going to have to be careful in how you approach the situation.

One of the most difficult times to motivate yourself to speak out about something is when you are not fueled by righteous indignation. When you are 99% sure and the other 1% of you is saying: "What if you are wrong?" You are wracked with self doubt and you don't want to offend a potentially innocent person. On the flip side, this is the best time to get what is bothering you off your chest because you are in the right frame of mind to have a real conversation. You have enough humility to admit that you were wrong, and you are caring enough to worry about how your approach is going to affect the other person.

What you choose to do is dependent upon the strength of the story you are telling yourself at that moment. So here is some advice for three different scenarios.

1. **No Evidence:** The one and only reason you think that your friend stole from you this time is through a process of elimination. In other words you don't really think it was her who stole it but there is no other explanation for your missing money.

   Advice: In this situation you should engage in a conversation about the missing money. Don't tell her what you think happened to the money but share the facts. If your friend is innocent something might jog her memory and she may be able to point you in the right direction. If she is guilty, she might display some body language or facial expressions that confirm your suspicions. You can say something like: "Last night I had two $50 bills in my purse, I left it in the dining room and when I searched for it this morning, it was gone. Has anything of yours gone missing?

2. **If you have quite a bit of evidence but you are afraid to be too direct:** You have several reasons to suspect that it was your friend because last night she said she didn't have any money but when you found out that your money was missing you took a sneaky look in her purse and found that she also had two $50 bills. You don't want to just outright accuse her because she has a bad temper and it could end up in a screaming match or worse.

Advice: In this situation, you have decided that there is too much risk involved in approaching your friend even though you are more than certain that she stole your money. However, if you don't say anything you will not be able to sleep. So since your money is missing, you now need a loan, you can ask your friend to lend you fifty bucks and see what she says, remember you already know that she has two fifty dollar notes in her purse.

In this scenario you are trying to be as indirect as possible but at the same time let her know that you are on to her. If she is an intelligent thief she will remember that she told you she didn't have any money last night. If she has forgotten what she told you and runs to get the $50 you have caught her out. Either way she loses. If she remembers telling you she has no money and then tells you again that she has no money after you ask for the loan, you know she is lying because you looked in her purse. If she loans you the money, she didn't remember that she told you she had no money and now all of a sudden she has money to give you. What you choose to do at either of these junctions is up to you.

3. **You have more enough evidence to confront her and nothing to lose:** In this situation you have several reasons to suspect her and you are not afraid of her reaction. The worst case scenario is that she denies it and decides that she no longer wants to be your friend. The only difference between the third and the second option is that you are giving her the opportunity to either admit it or deny it. Here are some suggestions for holding this conversation:

Advice: My first advice is that you don't say anything until you have come up with a plan B. Make a decision about what you will do if she denies stealing from you but you are still suspicious, she denies it and decides to end the friendship. Or she confesses that it was her.

You can start the conversation with an emphatic and sincere apology. "I am really concerned about something, and I feel awful bringing it up. But I know that if I don't say anything it is going to eat away at me and have a negative effect on our relationship. Can I talk to you about it?

You will now need to non-judgementally and carefully share your information with her. Take your time, and don't miss anything out. Then, very cautiously share your conclusion. In other words don't sound too confident in your suspicions. The conversation should go something like this: "The other night when we went out I had two $50 bills in my purse. I know that the money was there because when we got back in the house I was looking for my lighter and I folded the money up and tucked it into the small pocket in the inside and zipped it up. I left it on the counter and came back in the morning and it was gone. I have been thinking about this all day and I can't understand where this money could have gone to. Then when we went out to eat tonight, I noticed that you had two $50 in your purse."

Acknowledge your suspicion but be cautious. By now she knows what you are trying to imply. You now need to restore the safety of the conversation by:

1. Letting her know that you really hate the fact that you have come to this conclusion.

2. Let her know that if she made a mistake there are no hard feelings you still love her and you want to help her.

The conversation continues in the following manner: "I know this sounds like a really terrible thing for me to ask you but can you see why I would be thinking like this? Since I can't think of any other explanation about what happened to the money I thought I would speak to you instead of leaving it to fester. I want you to know that if you did make a mistake I still love you, we all make mistakes and I would never judge you."

How to Deal With a Kleptomaniac

You have noticed for some time now that your friend steals a lot. Even when you go out together, she has to steal something. You do a bit of research and you realize that there is a high possibility that she is a kleptomaniac. Here is how you can help her.

Consult a Healthcare Professional: The first thing you should do is contact a professional for advice. Kleptomaniacs often suffer from an underlying condition such as anxiety, bipolar or addiction. In some cases it might be necessary to prescribe an antipsychotic medication. Before you decide to step in and help, make sure you are well informed about the condition.

Approach Your Friend: It is important that your friend recognizes that they have a problem. If treatment is going to work they must have a desire to change. When you approach your friend, remember that this is a mental illness and it is a sensitive issue. You will need to be very compassionate and don't be judgemental towards them. The best way to treat kleptomania is through professional help. Let your friend know that you are willing to get them the help that they need.

Hobbies and Interests: One of the treatment suggestions will be that the kleptomaniac engages in pleasurable activities. As you have read, one of the symptoms of kleptomania is that they get a feeling of gratification once the theft has taken place. This feeling is the same as when a person takes part in activities that they like or when they exercise. Endorphins are released into the bloodstream which makes us feel good. Healthy activities need to replace the stealing in order to overcome her kleptomania. Since you are serious about helping your friend, you can go to the gym together, or play a sport together.

A Support Group: If your friend is not comfortable with seeking professional help just yet you can encourage her to join a support group. Support groups are often started by a former kleptomaniac. Everyone participating in the group has the same problem and so your friend won't feel isolated. Once she realizes that she is not the only person in the world suffering from this condition she will feel more comfortable seeing a trained professional.

Destroy all Stolen Goods: If your friend opens up enough and lets you know what she has stolen, you can both destroy the goods together. In this way she is destroying any connections she has that remind her of her desire to steal.

Be an Encouragement: Let your friend know that you intend on walking with her step by step throughout the healing process. Make sure that you encourage her vocally letting her know that you are proud of her and that she shouldn't give up.

How to Prevent Being a Target of Theft

Regardless of the reason why people steal a thief is an opportunist and if he knows he is not going to get away with stealing something he won't steal. There are things that you can do ensure that you don't continue to be a victim. Before I delve into that area, here is some interesting information.

Research has discovered that people who walk with their back straight are less likely to become a victim of robbery. A straight back gives the appearance of confidence and that they are in control. This alone reduces the desire of a thief to target an individual.

A thief looks for the easiest possible target, as stated they are opportunists. If a thief is on their way home and they had no intention of stealing anything but he walked past a house with the window wide open and a purse on a chair by the window, they are going to grab it.

A thief does not like obstacles, and so the more obstacles between them and the thing that they want to steal the more discouraged they will become. For example, a thief is not going to try and steal a car that has a wheel lock on it, that's just too much hassle to deal with. On the other hand, if you parked your car on a dark road with no street lights, few houses and no people walking around, a car thief is going to jump at the opportunity to steal your car.

If you leave your bag on the front seat of your car, a thief is going to get really excited about the prospect of there being a large amount of cash in the bag which will encourage them to break the window and take it.

When the person who steals is around you will need to take certain precautions. Regardless of the type of thief you are dealing with, every thief is an opportunist and if you want to help this person you are going to have to make it hard for them to steal.

- Make sure that all of your valuables are locked away before they arrive.

- Even if you have locked everything that you think is valuable away, you don't think like a thief and so you are not going to know what is appealing. When you are dealing with atypical theft behavior you are dealing with people who don't steal things of value but things that are symbolic; therefore, don't leave them alone not even for one second. The easiest way to do this is to make sure that someone else is with you when they arrive.

- Don't give personal information over the phone when the thief is around. This includes your social security number and account numbers.

- Shred all of your preapproved credit card offers.

- Keep your PIN's and passwords protected.

Conclusion

Life is not black and white, it never has been and it never will be there is always going to be a grey area. Nobody just wakes up one morning and decides they are going to start stealing, as you have read there are several reasons why people decide to take things that don't belong to them. Now, I am in no way condoning breaking the law but as we read in Victor's story, he didn't even understand why he was stealing until he had spoken to a psychiatrist. I personally have a lot of faith in the human race, I don't believe that anyone is inherently evil the circumstances of life can turn some people into monsters if they have not been trained to channel their pain in the right direction.

My philosophy in life is to treat others the way you want to be treated because you never know when the shoe is going to be on the other foot. I speak to a lot of homeless people when I am out and about. The other day I met a thirty year old man called Justin he has been homeless for the past year. While a student at the State University studying Anthropology he got a phone call that his entire family had been killed in a car crash. He went into a terrible state of shock and stopped speaking. He was admitted to a mental institution where it took 8 months of psychotherapy for him to start talking again. With no family and friends, when he was discharged he had no money and no place to live, he ended up living on the streets and has been homeless ever since.

Justin was extremely grateful that I had taken the time out to speak to him because in his own words "most people just walk past, they don't even look at me, I am invisible to them." I asked him one very important question, I asked him whether or not he used to stop and speak to homeless people when everything was going well in his life, I asked him if he could remember ever dropping a couple of dollars into the hands of a homeless person. He answered no to both questions. I didn't have to say anything else, he understood the point that I was trying to make.

While I will never encourage anyone to tolerate anyone treating them less than they deserve, you never know what life can bring your way. I am sure the Holocaust survivor Vincent did not know that he would one day become a victim of such horror. He had no idea that one day the consequences of what he went through would lead him to steal. I am certain that prior to the day he had stolen the kind of morals and values that he had would have caused him to loathe people who steal.

My point is this, as bad as it is to have the character traits of a coward, a thief, liar and a manipulator before you bang the hammer of judgement stop and think about what happened in this person's life that has turned them into this kind of person. Your compassion may lead them to take a good look at themselves and get the help that they need to become a better person.

Other books available by K.C. Smith on Kindle, paperback and audio:

Taking Destiny Steps: Learn How to Live Your Dreams

Everyone Screws Up: Learning To Forgive Your Stupid Mistakes and Recover With Grace and Humility

The Essence of Power: Learn How to Tap into Your Personal Power